The Stroke
of an *Artist*

The Journey of a Fitness Trainer
and a Stroke Survivor

by
Tracy L. Markley,
C.P.T, Biomechanics Specialist

Publish

Scrip
PUBLISHING

To Gary, the most dedicated and inspiring person I've ever known.

TABLE OF CONTENTS

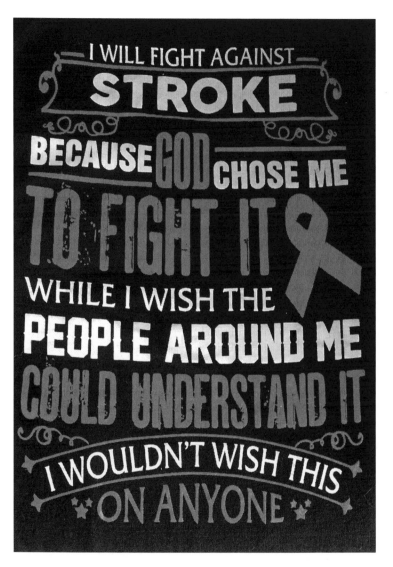

Gary said these exact words often. We were thrilled
to find it on a shirt one day and gave it to him.

FOREWORD

I came to know Tracy Markley over 10 years ago through FiTOUR®, a national education company for health and fitness professionals. We both present certification workshops for health and fitness professionals in various modalities of fitness, i.e., Pilates, group exercise, and personal training. Her vast knowledge and experience in the health and fitness industry far surpasses your regular run-of-the- mill personal trainer. Her clients love her because she can connect to them from her spirit and soul when she trains them. I was delighted when Tracy told me about her training experience with a stroke survivor, Gary, and how she was chronicling his exercise journey and his progress. Tracy's *The Stroke of An Artist* is an excellent story of hope for stroke survivors as well as a resource tool for health and fitness professionals helping stroke survivors. Her clever narrative about Gary's journey will take you on a roller coaster ride from apprehension through frustration and struggle to inspiration. Gary's story not only inspires others who struggle with physical setbacks, but it also encourages each person to test his/her physical boundaries even when outsiders may discourage it. In *The Stroke of An Artist*,

Tracy addresses the physical damages that a stroke survivor may experience and provides the very specific functional exercises utilizing various tools and props to help improve one's condition. The muscle illustrations and exercise demonstrations provide a useful visual for the reader to understand the practical application of functional movement.

Tag along with Tracy and Gary as they work together as a team towards victory over an initially un-cooperating body. I'm very excited to share this book with many of my clients who may be dealing with instability, loss of sensation, postural misalignment, and/or spatial awareness issues. *The Stroke of An Artist* will impact and transform the lives of stroke survivors and those who love them.

CarolAnn, M.S., CPT, CN

INTRODUCTION

Gary often would say to me, "Don't ever have a stroke; they suck." After hearing him say this more than a dozen times, I said to him, "You know, I think we need to write a book about your recovery and call it, *Dear Stroke, You Suck*." We both laughed, but I meant it. The idea to follow it through stuck strongly in my heart. Bringing hope to other stroke survivors was important to Gary. He knew how hard stroke recovery can be.

This is our story, shared with aspirations of bringing hope to stroke survivors to achieve the most progress possible in their recovery. For a long time, Gary repeated that he did not know what he would had done if we have not been working together. He would joke that he would just be home sitting around eating bonbons; then he would get back to being serious. He would say, "You know things and you really connect to what is going on. Others don't know what you know, do they?"

This is my journey as a personal fitness trainer about what I knew and what I learned during our time together that helped guide Gary to continually make progress, even at 34 months post stroke.

Gary was told when he left the first rehab in a wheel chair that he would be using it for the rest of his life. This rehab did tremendous work to get him as far along in his recovery as he had in the two months he was there. When he went home, he began more therapy with a physical therapist. This therapist told Gary he would get him out of the wheel chair, and he did.

Gary noticed as he was making continued progress in his own recovery that some other stroke survivors he had seen had either given up too soon or been told that their progress was limited. They essentially went back to trying to live their lives in their new, limited, "accepted" condition. Survivors may stop trying to make progress because their insurance only pays for a limited number of physical therapy sessions. This does not always mean their bodies have reached their full recovery potential. They may not know that there are fitness professionals who can help them when physical therapy ends.

As for the name of the book, you can see we didn't call it, *Dear Stroke, You Suck*. The reason is that Gary was an artist. He and I were sitting down talking a few months ago, and I asked him to describe to me what happens when he tries to paint now. He explained that in his head he wanted to paint a long, thin, stroke with the paintbrush, but his hand paints a short, thick stroke. I decided right then, *The Stroke of An Artist* would be the name of the book.

This book is not a statement that every stroke survivor will reach the same recovery achievements that Gary reached. There are different types of strokes. There are varying levels of impact, as well as other physical and medical conditions one may have. I was told that Gary had the worst kind of stroke possible and that not every male in his family who had a stroke survived, but Gary did. He told me he believed it was a miracle.

It is important to keep in mind as you read this book that the flow of events and subjects of the chapters are not written in order to follow as a step by step guide. His brain was trying to rewire itself. We trained as his brain and his progress guided us. There was no organized process.

We met at a gym in Florence, Oregon, but we both came from southern California. He was 17 years older than I, but we grew up going to the same beaches and surf spots and graduated from the same college. That familiarity helped us bond and gain a trust from day one.

CHAPTER 1

GARY WALKS INTO THE GYM

I had just finished training a client and was heading towards the front desk to see if my next client had arrived early. I was passing the cardio equipment when a man using a walker slowly approached me with what appeared to be his personal entourage by his side.

Earlier that week I had received a phone call from a woman asking me if I could train her brother who had suffered a stroke. As we approached one another, I knew this had to be Gary. We introduced ourselves. He had his sister, brother-in-law, and neighbor by his side. It was heartwarming to see someone with such a great support team.

We all chatted for a bit, there in the middle of the gym. I experienced how much love, support, and laughter he had around him. I thought to myself, "This is a special person." Right then a woman stood up next to us, reached out, touched Gary's arm and said to him, "You are going to get through this. Look at me. I had a stroke five years ago." She moved as though she never had a stroke. We all teared up, including Gary, which is very common after a stroke. It was as if it was meant to be for us all to meet that day, at that moment and speak right there at that very spot in the gym, right near her so she could give him encouragement and hope. It was one of the most remarkable and unforgettable first meetings with a client that I had experienced in my 20 years in the fitness industry. I knew at that very moment that Gary and I meeting was a God-send and that it was very important for us to meet.

Gary had suffered a massive stroke, six months before we met. He was unable to move his body at all. The doctors were not sure if he was going to survive. He was critical the first two weeks. He beat the odds.

CHAPTER 2

DEAR STROKE, YOU SUCK

G ary's body became a stranger to him. It no longer felt the same or moved the same. All the physical therapists and the equipment they used in his six months of therapy to get his body moving were amazing. They got him moving enough to be home, using a walker and a cane.

He felt powerless when our work first began. He was hesitant when his sister told him she thought that it would be good for him to join the gym and get a trainer to help him continue his progress. I found out about six months into working together that he hated gyms and did not want to do it. He told me he sat in the car as his sister went into the gym and enrolled him. She walked out to the car with two personal trainer business cards and said, "Do you want a man or a woman trainer?" He responded to her by saying, "I might as well have a woman if I have to do this." He had never been a member of a gym. He had a perception that it was all about having big muscles and egos. He thought if he had a male trainer, it would be a big, buff guy trying to make him do things he could not do.

Gary was six months post stroke the day we met. The stroke affected the right side of his body. He was using a walker and wearing a brace on his right leg. He also had a rotator cuff injury on his right side, had loss of peripheral vision on the right side, and experienced extreme weakness throughout the entire body. He had had a knee surgery on the right knee a couple of weeks prior to his stroke, and parts of his face and body were numb.

Gary could no longer drive a car. He lost all freedom and had to rely on others for things he used to do himself. He had been a distinguished artist from a young age. That was his profession and how he earned his income. Now he could no longer read, write, or do his artwork. He was unable to sign his name to the artwork that he had finished prior to his stroke. He had memory loss. He could not remember things like his birthday or how old he was. We met three days a week, and it took him almost two months to remember my name. Even though he had a great sense of humor and we laughed a lot about this, the memory loss was extremely frustrating for him. He did not remember many of the exercises we had done just a few days before, nor some of our conversations. He had lost the ability to bounce a ball, ride a bike, walk fast, run, walk backward and sideways, turn around, get down and up from the floor, and many other movements and activities. He lost his spatial awareness. (*See chapter on Spatial Awareness and Proprioception.*)

10

He no longer felt safe when stepping backward or turning around to change direction when walking. These essential movements that we do every day are ones he hoped to regain.

At this time, I had trained approximately a dozen clients who were in stroke recovery. Gary would be the first to begin training with me in such a fragile state. I knew it was extremely important to focus on his core and stabilizing structure of his body as soon as possible.

This was an exceptionally challenging goal for us to tackle because the software of his body (the brain) had malfunctioned due to the stroke. The brain's ability to reorganize and rewire itself is known as neuroplasticity. A simple way to describe this would be when the brain was trying to get a message to a specific part of the body to make a movement, but the message could not get through because the wires in the messaging system were not working properly. The brain now has to create new pathways to get the message sent and received properly as it did before the stroke. For example, if you were following directions on a road map to travel from point A to point B, and you run into roadblocks, you have to figure out alternative routes to get to your destination. In many cases, the brain rebuilds these new pathways. The experience of Gary and me working together clearly showed us that we cannot predict which new pathways will appear, the time frame they will appear, nor the order in which they will appear. We were continually reminded while sharing this journey together that there is no time frame or limits on this process.

He often felt clumsy, awkward, and frustrated, but he was filled with a lot of determination to beat all the challenges the stroke presented him. He seemed to have this inner joy, and people liked being around him. Even at our first training session together, I could easily get him to laugh.

He would talk about feeling normal again. I would explain that he would have a new normal. In this process, one grieves the "old self" with thoughts and feelings of waiting for it all to come back. However now there is a "new self" physically developing that may never be the same. We had no idea what could come back nor how long it would take. A part of the self is grieving the loss of the body familiarity and the loss of who it was. Those feelings, combined with the feelings of not knowing physically how much better one will become, is quite a struggle in itself.

He slurred his speech for quite some time after the stroke, but I don't remember taking much notice of it. I think it was mostly gone when I met him, but he said it was there. He knew how he spoke and sounded before his stroke; I did not. On several occasions when I was with him when he met another member at the gym, he would laugh and say, "I swear I am not drunk. I normally don't talk like this. I had a stroke."

There were many dynamics to his recovery. Communication, focus, and being present in the moment were essential for both of us.

CHAPTER 3

GARY TOOK A CHANCE

In our first personal training session together, I had to assess him carefully by taking him through some functional movements to see and feel exactly how we could begin safely. As with all my clients, and especially important in Gary's case, not only did I need to know what his body was able to do, I needed to know what it was unable to do. He had a hard time just getting up and down from sitting in a chair. His arms and legs were extremely weak. I needed to know his ability to control his stabilizing muscles.

He had his neighbor with him, so we took him over to a stability ball. While safely holding the ball and with his neighbor's assistance, we sat him on the ball to see if he had any control or stabilizing ability to hold himself up. He was exceptionally weak, and he would have slid off the ball to the floor if we had not assisted him. This was one significant sign that we were on the right path by beginning with strengthening the stabilizing muscles of the body, so we could get them strong and functioning at their best as soon as possible. We then took him over to a low therapy table where he could sit down. I gave him a Bender® Ball to put between his knees. I had him gently squeeze (flex inner thighs) and release the ball between his legs without dropping it. This was to determine if he could recruit and flex the adductors of the hip. He was able to do it slowly. Of course, the left leg was stronger than the right leg since the stroke had affected his right leg. He also had a harder time controlling the movement of the right leg. The purpose of this exercise was also to strengthen the pelvic floor and adductors as he focused on using the muscles that helped him sit upright. I told him my goal was to get him to advance from sitting on the bench to sitting on the big ball to perform this exercise. He looked at me as if I were insane, then smiled, and said, "Okay." He told me he could not understand how that could happen, but he said he trusted me. That was heartwarming, and I felt honored that he trusted me so quickly.

I showed him some illustrations of a few muscles and explained the importance of making them stronger so he could function in movement for standing and walking. He took a copy of the illustrations home the following week to help remind him why he was doing the exercises and to be consciously aware of the muscles he was to focus on doing his homework. I find if clients have a visual plus an understanding of why they are doing the exercises, it serves them a greater purpose.

I began teaching him how to engage his core muscles at his first workout. The best way I would explain it to him was for him to visualize and try to feel as if he were putting on a belt or a tight pair of jeans and zipping up the zipper to his rib cage or sternum. My goal was to get him to connect to the deepest abdominal muscle, the transverse abdominal, and the pelvic floor. I wanted to get his brain communicating with the muscles in his stabilizing system as soon as possible. (*See chapter on Rebuilding the Body and Pathways.*)

In the muscle illustrations I showed him, I had a green picture of the transverse abdominal muscle. I would say, "Zip up that green muscle." We would laugh, but he would do it. It would only last for a few seconds, and then we had to repeat it again.

As we continued in our next workout sessions, I had him slowly walking on the treadmill for a few minutes while holding on to keep the locomotion of walking repeated and practiced as much as possible while focusing on his walking gate and feet placements. He was also doing this in his homework. Repeating the movement the body is trying to perfect helps the brain build new pathways for that movement. Consistency and repetition are important!

For several months, he was unable to do any exercises that required him to get up and off the floor. We continued to work on his stabilizing muscles by sitting up on the therapy table and consciously connecting to those muscles. He combined this movement while he did the exercises with the Bender® Ball between his knees and trying to focus on the leg muscles at the same time. This may seem easy, but it was a difficult task in his case. He did this sitting at the end of the therapy bench until he was able to do it sitting on the big ball.

I was continually directing him. I sounded something like this, "Sit up tall, keep the feet flat on the ground, sit up tall, watch that foot, sit up tall. Stay engaged, it will help you sit up tall, don't forget to squeeze the ball, sit up tall." We laughed a lot

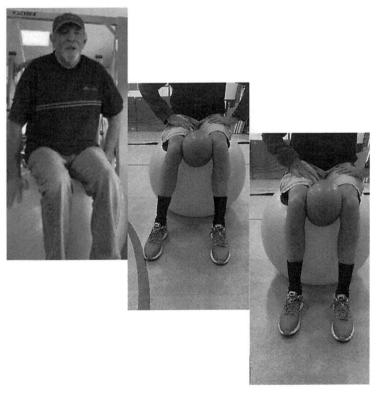

through this, but he had to retrain the brain to multitask during movements. I told him sit up tall or stand up tall at least 50 times a session. His brain needed to keep communicating with the stabilizing muscles whenever his body did a movement. I played the role of a "second brain" to remind his brain to communicate to his body. His body would not establish functional movement if over time he went to move a limb and the stabilizing muscles turn off instead of firing up.

It did not take long before he was able to sit on the Swiss ball next to the therapy bench, where he can hold on. In time, we moved the ball away from the bench but kept him near the bench to hold onto if he needed to. A couple of weeks into our journey together, I showed him the balance disc and told him he would be standing on that soon. I showed him what he would be doing. He looked at me as if I were crazy, then said, "Can I try it now?" I took  him to the squat rack so he had a bar to hold onto and had him stand on the balance disc. It was not easy and of course it felt awkward, but he did it. Standing on the balance disc stimulates the central nervous system, strengthens abdominal and spine muscles, helps train the body to balance in movement, and I feel it assists in resetting the body's internal bracing system. He understood the good it would do him. He bought a balance disc and took it home to begin practicing it daily at home, too.

I showed him how to do a ball squat against the wall with the big ball. I asked him if he thought he could do it, and again he looked at me as if I were nuts and laughed; then he wanted to try. I had him do a ball squat on a wall with something next to him to grab onto, if needed. He was able to perform a couple squats. After a few weeks of doing it with me, he was able to do more reps and he began doing them at home daily as well. This was an exercise he took to quickly and remembered. Within the first two months of training, he was sitting on the big ball, standing on the balance disc while holding onto something, and he was doing ball squats on the wall.

Gary also had that rotator cuff injury on the right side. This was not my main focus at this time. During our time working together, he saw a physical therapist for this injury, but it was slow to heal. It did not seem to be getting better for quite some time. He went to physical therapy twice for this during our training together. The second time, it finally worked. I strongly believe it worked because by that time his core was strong enough to maintain better posture so that he was able to hold his shoulder girdle in proper alignment. This allowed the therapy exercises to ultimately work.

About a month before his stroke, Gary also had a knee surgery on the right knee. I am unclear as to what took place with the knee during rehab. He was left with an unstable, hyper extended knee on the same side of the body the stroke had affected.

There was a lot to process and take in for both of us in the first workout session. I knew for sure that focusing on stabilization and stimulating the nervous system were the most essential tasks for the whole body to regain its normal abilities as much as possible until he was able to gain enough stability to add more functional movements safely.

CHAPTER 4

COMMUNICATION IS ESSENTIAL

It is crucial to have clear communication between my client and me. I regularly ask clients questions to be sure they are feeling the specific exercise where the exercise was intended to be felt.

This is important. I find at times clients may appear to be doing an exercise correctly, but may be feeling it in a different place than I planned, for various reasons. They may need to correct their form, but they can't. I need to know if it is because the client does not understand or their body cannot physically do what I am asking. For example: a client is feeling their neck while doing a bicep curl because he is tensing his neck and shoulders internally but not enough for me to see his shoulders raise up or when a client is in perfect form for a squat but their knee begins to hurt. In order for me to serve the clients the best I can, these things are necessary for me to know. I also need to know how hard or easy an exercise is for them.

When a client has numbness in half of his body and the brain cannot connect to what the body is doing or feeling, it can make the communication a bigger challenge. Gary could not understand what it meant to "feel fatigue" in a muscle from working out. This is when most of us know our limit. There is a difference between muscle fatigue and a muscle that is numb and not getting all the messages from the brain to perform at its best. He told me that besides surfing, he never exercised on purpose. He had not worked out with weights nor been in a gym, so this was a foreign language to him, plus combined with the stroke effects.

This is also where I felt like I had to be his second brain to help him stay safe. I had to ask questions repeatedly to make sure he did not get up from a machine or the ball and collapse to the floor because the right leg gave out. It was often difficult for him to know and then explain what he was feeling or not feeling. He tried though. He would feel bad sometimes because he could not communicate to me what he wanted to say, but I understood. At times, the brain would not process a word he wanted to say as quickly as it did before the stroke. He understood very well that his right leg would feel heavy and numb. He was now combining those sensations with exercising that leg and trying to decipher the sensation of exercising. It was brain overload at times.

With this in mind, I also had to determine if he was overdoing exercises at home or if the exercises we were doing that day were extra hard. Like everyone, his body needed to keep moving daily, but not overdo it. He also needed proper recovery. Finding that balance when you cannot feel all the sensations in your body is quite difficult. I asked him at each visit what he did the day before at home and often, in the first six months, he could not remember. If I saw him having a hard time mentally or physically in a session, I would ask again what he had done at home, and then he may or may not remember.

Communication is vital, but it was difficult sometimes. He was remarkably in tune with what he wanted to express, and he wanted to be as clear as possible with his answer. However, it took sometimes five to ten minutes for him to do so because of the stroke. It was usually when he was trying to express the sensation of what the body was either feeling, or not feeling, during or after an exercise. When it took a long time to get a specific word I would often ask questions, hoping it would help his brain think of the word by me coming at it from another angle. This was okay and mandatory as far as I was concerned. It would have been unfair to Gary and his progress if I just assumed something I thought he was trying to tell me.

As we progressed together, I began taking out my cell phone and taking pictures or videos to help us communicate. One example is when we were working on his foot drop and turn out while walking. I would video his feet from the front of the treadmill or him walking down the hall so he could see what needed to be changed or what had changed. He put a mirror in front of his treadmill at home so he could see his legs and feet while he walked on the treadmill. Another example as he progressed and was able to perform a plank exercise was that he was not always understanding my verbal directions to get into proper form. If I showed him a picture of him doing a plank, then showed him me doing a plank in proper position, he then could more clearly relate to the directions I was giving. This process of communication was fabulous not only for the communication aspect but we were able to use them later on in his journey so he could see how far he had progressed from earlier times.

He did not like looking in the mirror. One reason being his perception of where he was in space was off. He had a loss of peripheral vision on the right side. The message his brain sent for movement was struggling. If he tried to watch himself in the mirror and make the movements, it complicated things even more. He was best off if he stayed focused on the movement he was trying to achieve. Even later in his journey as he had achieved great progress, I continually found that he still would not look at himself in the mirror. He spent 65 years knowing who he was when he looked at himself, but after the stroke, he saw himself differently. This is very common. We had discussions about this. He would say he did not understand why. I shared with him that there was a time in my life where I was very ill for a few years and when I looked in the mirror, I did not see me. I saw a stranger and I felt like a stranger, in my own body. He responded with, "Exactly."

There were at least a dozen times during our work together when he would achieve a great gain in progress, and he would leave the gym so happy and thankful. He would return to the gym after the weekend, and he would seem down. I would ask him what was going on. He would say he was frustrated and feeling down because he was not making progress. I think this would happen because he was still unable to do things he used to do before the stroke. I would get my phone and show him the videos and pictures of his progress that he had made. He would light up, get a big smile on his face, and say thank you. Communication of his emotional well-being was also important.

As we communicated about anything we were doing, he and I both listened to one another and to our own instincts. We asked questions of one another. This was very important. We developed a great communication between us.

CHAPTER 5

REBUILDING THE BODY AND PATHWAYS

G ary needed to feel stable and safe in movement again as soon as he could. In this chapter, I highlight some of the principles I have found to be the foundations to a healthy, functioning body. This is the longest, most complex, and very important chapter in this book. This may be a helpful chapter for fitness professionals who are having stroke survivors come to them for training as well as any client needing to improve balance, stability, and regain the awareness of where his or her body is in space.

I have obtained knowledge from many great teachers in the past 20 years working in the fitness industry. My teaching methods are a combination of knowledge gained from all of these teachers as well as my experience to what has worked with my clients.

Scientific research has shown that in a healthy body the brain sends a message to the balancing system before it sends a message to the legs and the arms for movement. This is the brain telling the body to stabilize and support the body because it is ready to move. It also means we recruit from the core of the body moving outwards to move. This is known as a sensory-generated motor pattern. With this in mind, because of a stroke, remember the brain is already having a hard time getting messages to the body for proper movement. The brain is trying to create new pathways of communication because the old pathways are not working properly. It makes sense to me, that if the stabilizing muscles are weak and not functioning to their full potential it could cause the rebuilding of pathways to the limbs to be more difficult to achieve.

There is another important reason I began strengthening the core and stabilizing muscles. The transverse abdominal muscle, the multifidus muscle, diaphragm, and the pelvic floor muscles are all on the same neuromuscular loop. This means it's best if all muscles are functioning properly in order for each to perform its job individually and as a team. My studies taught if the transverse muscle is weak, the pelvic floor, the multifidus, and the diaphragm cannot gain their proper strength to work at their best potential to perform the job they need to do for a healthy, functioning body. I have found all of this to be true.

The Transverse Abdominis

The transverse muscle is the deepest of the abdominal muscles. A critical function of this muscle is to stabilize the lower back and pelvis before movements. It is the deepest abdominal muscle. This muscle wraps around to act like a corset. When engaged, it also pulls the belly in and provides support to the thoracolumbar fascia. It is the main stabilizer of the shoulder girdle, the head, neck, pelvis, and lower extremities.

Gary had rounded shoulders and poor posture, and it could not have corrected if his transverse muscle maintained the weakness that it had. He needed to build a strong transverse muscle along with the other stabilizing muscles to hold his body strongly upright so he could achieve the posture of stacking his shoulders over the hips. If the head is upright and balanced over the shoulders, we have better balance. He also needed the stability in his pelvis and hips so the lower limbs and joints could gain strength and function in proper alignment and perform properly for safe movements.

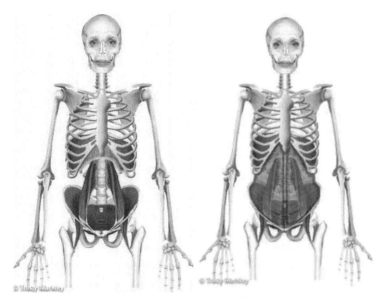

The Multifidus Spinae

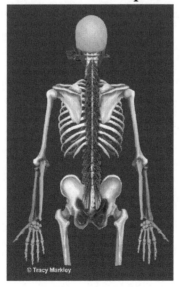

The multifidus is a small but powerful muscle. It is the main stabilizing muscle of the spine. This muscle takes pressure off the vertebral discs so the body weight can be distributed throughout the spine. If this is weak, you will also have weakness in the low back. The multifidus begins to activate before the body moves to protect the spine. It is part of the stabilizing system in the body. Gary needed this muscle stronger, too. Performing various exercises combined with the Swiss ball, balance disc and BOSU® ball is how Gary gained a stronger multifidus. The strength and gains of better posture and balance that Gary achieved came as this muscle, the transverse and pelvic floor all became balanced in strength and working together as a team keeping that neurological loop in a cycle of strength and communication.

We needed to get his small muscles near the vertebrae to be activated harmoniously. These muscles are postural muscles. Having Gary work with the balance disc daily, especially in the beginning, was important. Exercising on an unstable surface, such as the balance disc and the BOSU® ball, stimulates the central nervous system which is the brain and the spinal cord. It strengthens muscles, ligaments, and activates and strengthens all the small muscles along the spinal column. (*See Disc and BOSU® Ball Chapter.*) When Gary focused and stood as upright as he could each time he stood on the balance disc at the gym and at home, he was working on strengthening his core and postural muscles.

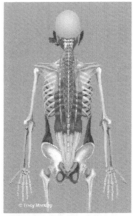

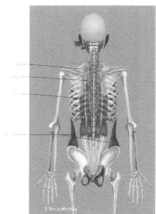

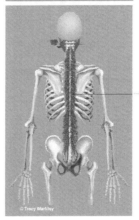

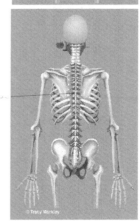

The Pelvic Floor Muscles

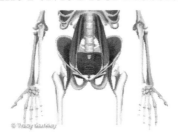

The pelvic floor muscles work as stabilizers of the abdominal and pelvic organs. The pelvic floor muscles and the gluteus muscles (buttocks muscles) are made to work and move in opposite directions. One must be able to engage the pelvic floor without engaging the gluteus muscles in order to obtain optimal core strength. These two muscles must be separated in the brain and nervous system for overall whole body functioning. This plays a role in preventing back issues, and I don't want to build back issues in any client. The transverse muscle must be strong in order for the pelvic floor to get strong and function properly since they are on the same neuromuscular loop.

When Gary did certain exercises, I would tell him to engage the pelvic floor then to visualize and feel like he is zipping up a zipper from the pelvic floor to his rib cage or sternum. The more conscious and present he was when doing this, the better chance subconsciously these muscles would contract in everyday movements when needed without him thinking about it.

This was important while sitting on the big ball and standing on the balance disc during our first few months together to help get his center and core strong to stabilize him. This was also important for Gary as he progressed into mat Pilates exercises.

The pelvic floor works close to the diaphragm as well. If you sit or stand in good alignment and focus on engaging the pelvic floor, you can feel that the diaphragm pulls slightly towards the pelvic floor as the pelvic floor lifts slightly upwards towards the diaphragm. There is a difference between doing a Kegel and engaging the pelvic floor. It is also important to be able to engage the pelvic floor without engaging the buttocks (glutes) for the inner unit and stabilizing system in the body to work efficiently.

Thoracolumbar Fascia

The thoracolumbar fascia supports the back muscles and helps them achieve the ability to move the body. It is made up of strong fibers and helps channel forces of movement as the back muscles contract and relax. The nerves to these muscles also cross through this fascia. This fascia goes deep to the spine and is made of three layers. It is essential for contralateral motions like walking. It works with the latissimus dorsi (lats) to coil the core of the body.

When the thoracolumbar fascia is supported, it allows all the muscles that connect to it to function better. These muscles include the gluteus maximus, latissimus dorsi, trapezius, erector spinae, quadratus lumborum, psoas, transverse and internal obliques. It helps bridge the muscles of the back to the muscles of the abdominal wall. This fascia helps integrate the movements of the upper body with the lower body.

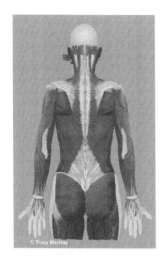
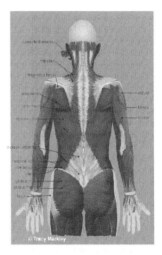
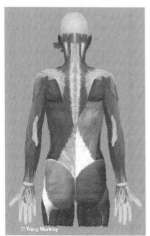
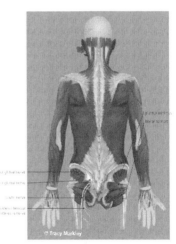

If you look at the above illustration you will see how the opposite latissimus dorsi muscle and the opposite glute fibers run the same way and flow into this fascia. They all work together functionally to move the body. All the muscles that connect to this fascia need to be strengthened so the body systems that work together for movement can all flow functionally. Also, the illustrations show just some of the nerves that come into the fascia and throughout the body.

I could write a complete chapter on fascia, but for now here is a brief description of fascia. Fascia is a continuous structure that surrounds and intermingles tissues and structures throughout the body. It varies in density and thickness. Nerves and blood vessels also run through fascia. The brain is sending messages for movement which includes the fascia. Training Gary with the knowledge of this was important while choosing which exercises were the best for him. He rarely sat at the gym machines to train. Fascia is also interconnected with the structures it surrounds. The health and mobility of fascia plays a huge role for the body to have heathy movement, and to avoid pain and injury. There have been ongoing studies on fascia and its mandatory importance for the body to move.

The Psoas (Iliopsoas) Muscle

The psoas is an extremely important muscle for proper function. It is also a muscle in the center of the body. It lies deep underneath the transverse abdominal muscle. While the transverse muscle is known as the deepest abdominal muscle, the psoas is the known as a deep back muscle. Often it can be referred to as the iliopsoas. This is when the psoas and the iliacus muscle are being grouped together. The psoas muscle is the only muscle

in the back that crosses over the hips and attaches at the front of the body. It attaches at the last thoracic vertebrae and to four of the five lumbar vertebrae and at the femur, the upper thigh bone. Some refer to this muscle as the magic muscle. It flexes the hip and externally rotates the hip joint.

Gary needed all these deep core muscles strengthened before I tried to get him to do a lunge or a squat without holding on for support. Many people perform these exercises when they have a weak and shortened psoas muscle and weakness deep in the core, and they end up with lower back injuries. Gary had to rebuild his body

from the inside out for safety to avoid injuries and to gain proper functioning throughout his whole body.

I asked my incredible illustrator Susan if she could make the psoas muscle doing a lunge on us, and she did. Isn't it wonderful?

Some people refer to this area of the body as the trunk while others may refer to it as the core. However one may view it, this is the center of the body and the idea here is to emphasize the importance of it to be strong, stable, and functioning as a team with the rest of the body. If you look at each illustration in this chapter, you can see just how important it is to have the center, the core of the body, strong and stable. Gary needed all these muscles strong and working together as a team for proper movement in order for his body to rebuild the best it could and to achieve the most he could in his stroke recovery.

Chapter 6

The Body Was Made to Move

The body was made to move. The body needs to have some movement every day to help it regain what it was before the stroke. What we do most is what our body is trained to do best. If we sit more, we become better sitters. If we move more, our bodies become better at movement.

Gary did some physical activity every day either at home, at the gym, or both. I feel this was an essential part of his great progress. All the knowledge of stroke recovery can only do so much unless the body is moving daily. He began to come to the gym six days a week. In the first year, he was with me three times a week in one-hour private sessions. The days he did not see me for an appointment, I found him at the gym and checked on him. In the beginning months, he would just walk on the treadmill, do some ball squats, and go stand on the balance disc while holding on and practicing letting go until he did not need to hold on anymore.

For over a year, he needed supervision for many exercises he did with me. It took him quite some time to connect to feeling the good form for safety if I was not with him to coach him each time. It is essential that the body trains in proper form so it does not create imbalances around joints in movements. There is less stress on the body physiology when the biomechanics are functioning properly. Physiology focuses on the systems and organs of the body and their functions. Gary needed to build functional movement habits, not compromising habits. On his own at the gym, he was limited with what he could do for a while.

He moved everyday doing some sort of exercise. This is very important to understand because it played a large roll in his progress. I share these photos below to show what he achieved because he made sure he moved in some way using the exercises he learned and walking every day.

These three pictures were taken at approximately two and one-half years post stroke. I mentioned in the chapter on communication that we started using pictures and videos to help communicate and connect to him seeing his progress.

He was working on his running. When he ran, his right arm wanted to curl up again, and his foot wanted to drop, too. His brain was not quite ready to keep up with the running. This was a great improvement compared to a year prior, when he did not feel safe when he attempted to run.

In the middle picture, he is standing on the BOSU® ball bouncing a basketball, and it was fabulous! A year prior, he had just begun to stand on the BOSU® ball, and he had to hold on to a bar. He was unable to bounce a ball with any control the first year I worked with him. Bouncing a ball takes great cognitive skills. Standing on the BOSU® ball as he is balancing and remaining focused on bouncing the basketball, controlling the height of the bounce and keeping control of it takes tremendous focus. All this is happening while the nervous system is being fired up. This shows incredible progress in Gary's stroke recovery.

His right knee at this time of this picture was finally very stable. Up until just the last two months of his training, his knee fell out to the side unless he focused very consciously to control it. He had me repeat to him every few minutes to fix the knee. It was awesome when he was nearing three years post stroke and almost all the feeling was coming back in that leg. By this time, he had been using battle ropes for a couple months, which were hard work, but he was able to do them. He also was able to stand on the BOSU® ball and do the battle ropes.

One important reason he was able to make these three great gains was because he rebuilt his body from the inside out as his brain continued to make the new pathways which guided us to the next step, and he moved every day. Even when his body needed to recover, he still took a walk. On the rare occasion he had to miss a class or session at the gym, he would tell me that he felt he would lose everything he gained if he stopped.

CHAPTER 7

TREADMILL AND WALKING

Gary was already walking very slowly on the treadmill at home holding on safely when we began working together. This was to be part of his program with me at the gym as well. Since he had a brace on his leg and his foot dropped and turned out when he walked, he was determined to beat this and get back to his normal body.

He was already walking on the treadmill at home every hour for ten to fifteen minutes daily, slowly, while holding on. I showed him a study from the Cleveland Clinic that stated walking was one of the best things to do after a stroke. I asked him why he was doing it, and he said because it drove him crazy to sit and do nothing. He just knew to move more made better sense than sitting if he wanted his body to get better. I told him how cool it was for him to just feel that and to follow his inner guidance.

One of the things we focused on with the treadmill was for him to be present and conscious and to keep the right foot pointing forward as much as he could. This required being focused every second on his foot placement when he walked.

He walked with his cane for the first several months I worked with him. Then he would carry it with him in case he needed it. I don't remember the exact timing in recovery he stopped using it completely. I know he was still keeping it with him at 17 months post stroke when he was beginning Pilates. He was using a walker at night at home for about a year until he felt safe getting up out of bed in the dark and moving around.

An important impact of the walking gait is stabilization and strength of the pelvic girdle, which leads us right back to the core and the deep stabilizing muscles of the body. When all that is stable, the lower limbs will be more stable, and can build their strength for functional movement at its best while avoiding injury. Combined with the partial leg extension three days a week, (see chapter 12) we continued to do daily work on the balance disc and Swiss ball.

Walking backward and backward movements

Walking backward might seem silly, but it's good for you physically and mentally. We take steps backward often in our daily activity. Walking backward enhances the sense of body awareness. It increases body coordination and movement of the body in space. Research has shown walking backward improves the walking forward skills. It is said to sharpen your thinking skills, enhance cognitive control, and put the senses into overdrive. This movement also puts less strain on the knees and requires less range of motion from the knee joints.

About six months into our work together, I had Gary try to walk backward so I could understand where his ability with it was at that time. He looked very unstable and said he felt unsafe, so we stopped. I knew we would come back to it at another time. We tried it again after he spent time working on the BOSU® ball with exercises stepping up and down and really focusing on foot placement as he placed his feet exactly where he wanted them to land on the BOSU® ball as well as when he stepped back off to the floor.

On several occasions in this book I mention having awareness as to where the "body is in space." I don't do it to be annoyingly repetitive. It is very important. It is important for athletes to practice and train with focused awareness of where their body is in space for function, speed, and agility. They gain better balance, speed and quicker reaction time which are highly important skills for sports, especially fast-moving sports. Stroke survivors need to regain these skills for everyday life movements. Gary could not walk backward yet because he did not have the awareness of where his feet were in space, especially the right foot. When he tried to walk backward it was like the right foot was going into the unknown. He had no control of foot placement backward and that leg was not stable to hold him up while the left leg stepped backward. The right leg and foot still had numbness as well. Think of how many times a day you actually step backward in daily activities like taking clothes out of the dryer, opening a door toward you, picking things up, turning around, approaching a chair to sit down, and many others.

I found that stepping up and off the BOSU® ball while holding on to the bar helped him reconnect to the awareness of his feet in space. The brain and body are trying to come into awareness together in placement of the foot as one foot steps up and as one steps back down. The brain is programming in both directions to how high the BOSU® ball dome is and the distance from standing behind the dome and reaching to the top. The brain has to calculate and send a message to the body to step backward off the dome back to the floor as it is also calculating and sending messages to how far the foot has to be lifted up and then placed to clear the dome in stepping back far enough. This may seem easy, but when you lose this awareness in movement, it takes intense concentration. Gary also had to regain feeling safe again in such movements. The more conscious he was in movements, the more the subconscious rebuilt the skill.

When he initially went to step up on the dome of the BOSU® ball, he had no control to put the foot right where he wanted it to go. It was about two years after the stroke when this came into complete recovery for this movement. I used to say, "Move your foot right/left or forward/back," and it would take time for his brain to process what I said. Then it took time for his brain to get the message to his legs and feet for the movement. It took several attempts and wiggling the foot side to side to get the foot placed where he wanted it. Once someone feels safe and in control in this specific exercise, walking backward can be attempted safely. I was happy for him when he gained back complete control of placing that right foot where he wanted. I was even happier for him when he was able to do it without thinking about it. He pushed through and practiced it every day he could.

One day he was holding onto the squat rack bar to set up for a lunge, and he placed that right foot in one easy flowing movement exactly where he wanted it. A week prior it was still an effort. From that point forward it was no longer a struggle. Each time he had a great gain like this he would stop and say the most sincere thank you to me. When he would get ready to leave the gym on those days, he would come find me and to thank me again. Many times, he was so touched he had tears in his eyes when he said thank you; then I would tear up too. It was always great when we ended a training session where a great gain had happened. I would tell others at the gym who knew him, and they would cheer him on.

Gary used to take big, wide circles of steps in order to turn around. I remember the day he turned around normally. He lit up and said, "Did you see that"? I excitingly said, "Yes I did; that is so cool!"

I read studies that suggest having a client walk backward on a treadmill to help increase awareness and foot placement, but I am not comfortable with that. I feel walking backward on a treadmill belt can be unsafe for most clients. I suggest having clients do it on the floor in front of a mirror so they can see and feel their foot placement. Since he hated looking in the mirror, I had to repeatedly tell him to watch just his feet and his walking gait in the mirror. He was nearing about the two-year post stroke mark when he began safely walking backward across the basketball court at the gym.

I feel strongly that clients in such fragile states must have their core stabilizing muscles, as explained in chapter two, before attempting to go backward. Stability and safety are essential.

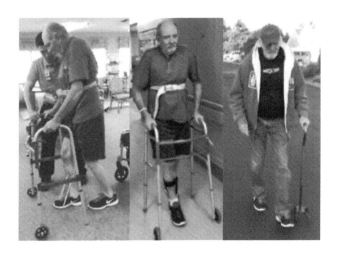

Walking Across the BOSU® balls

When he was ready and stable, I lined up three BOSU® balls on the floor. As usual, when I showed him what I was planning for him to do, he looked at me like I was nuts and laughed. Then he asked, "Can I try it now?"

I had him step onto one, and when he felt balanced and stable, he would step from one to the other. This is extremely good for balance, stability, walking, awareness of feet placement, quick reaction time, the neurological system, strengthening the core, pelvic and leg muscles, focus, and more. In time, he began to step from one ball to the other and do a squat and then step to the next. He even began to turn around on the last ball and go back across them instead of stepping on the floor to turn around. This took months and months of practice and continued throughout his training with me.

CHAPTER 8

HOMEWORK

Gary was eager to heal. His wife would set him up with different things such as picking up small objects like pins and placing them in a bowl. They worked on his reading and writing skills. He had to learn to sign his name again. He had those paintings waiting to be signed. He was walking on the treadmill slowly at home for a few minutes every hour. In time, he worked his way up to 15-20 minutes almost every waking hour. He did this on his own. He was following his own instinct and he was determined to beat this. He walked and walked. Once he got to the point where he could stand on the balance disc safely without me coaching him, he added that to his homework as well. When he was ready to walk without his cane, he began to walk around his neighborhood several times a day.

When we were trying to do some work with him seeing colors and peripheral vision, I suggested that he get a Simon® game from the 80s. It is the game that has four big buttons, green, red, yellow, and blue. Each button lights up, and one has to remember and repeat the pattern by hitting the buttons to a certain speed. This is wonderful for the brain, memory, and gaining quicker reaction time. I thought that possibly if he also did this on an angle utilizing peripheral vision it may help him regain his own peripheral vision back.

Gary was doing ball squats with me at the gym. As soon as he felt safe and could manage staying in proper position on his own, he bought a Swiss ball for his home and began doing them at home, almost daily, as well.

I expressed previously that at times it would get difficult to determine if he was overdoing physical activities when I was not around him. He would forget in the beginning exactly what he did. When he remembered he would tell me he walked on the treadmill at home and did the ball "things" on the wall. This meant ball squats against the wall. We often laughed in our communication. He did not mean to forget things; it was part of the stroke effects.

He never stopped taking his few daily walks around his neighborhood and he did some sort of exercise daily to keep himself moving.

CHAPTER 9

SPATIAL AWARENESS & FEELING SAFE IN MOVEMENTS

Proprioception - Being Aware of Where Your Body is in Space.

Spatial awareness is the ability to be conscious of oneself in space. It's to be mindful of where your body is and how much room you have around it and knowledge of the distance of objects in your surroundings. It is also referred to as proprioception; the placement of the body in relation to the things around it. It is the discernment of organized knowledge of the objects around oneself, in relation to the given space at any time, either being still or when there is a change of position. It is relating to the height and depth of the objects around you, such as having to step over something on the floor when you are walking through a room. You must be able to relate to the height of the object you need to step over so your foot lifts high enough and steps far enough out before landing back on the floor to clear the object. Spatial awareness is a complex cognitive skill. We learn this skill as children. It must be relearned in many cases after a stroke as was the case with Gary.

Without adequate proprioception from the trunk and legs, it is difficult simply to walk into a room and sit down in a chair. Example, when you enter a room and are aware of how far to walk to the chair, the brain calculates the distance and the feet walk accordingly. The body starts taking smaller steps when needed, as well as adjusting the speed of each step as it approaches the chair to turn around. Now the brain calculates the turn and the size of steps and the direction of the steps required to place the body in the right position to prepare to sit. It then calculates the distance, height, and where the seat of the chair is in space as it coordinates with where the body is in space before it lowers the body to sit down safely. The brain directs the body so it knows where it is in space to guide it down into sitting position in the chair without missing the chair and falling to the floor.

When Gary was at 30 months post stroke, he walked up to a chair and sat down normally. I asked him, "Do you realize what you just did?" He said "No. What?" I shared with him the huge value of what he just gained back, and I mimicked what he used to do. He used to walk slowly towards the chair. He would come to a stop, hold on to the chair, slowly turn around, and sit down as he was holding on. Then he would slowly slide himself back into the chair. We did a re-enactment video of this on my YouTube channel.

After his stroke, it was difficult for him to decipher the left from right and confused positional languages when given verbal directions such as forward, back, right, or left. This can be very common after a severe stroke. This makes it hard for a stroke victim to follow directions that use such language.

One day out of the blue, he stopped and explained to me that he knew there was the road with cars driving on it outside the gym and that there were people around him at the gym, but only because he knew it, not because he "saw" or "felt" them around him. The sense of his surroundings was not there. He was actually describing his loss of spatial awareness. I have expressed how incredibly in tune he was and it was amazing how he explained this to me.

I remember the day Gary began getting back his spatial awareness. He was at 18 months post stroke. He was standing on the balance disc when he stepped off the disc and said, "Wait, I need to share something." He made a small movement with his arms close to his body as if he were making a small circle around himself with his hands and said, "It's like my world used to stop here." Then he reached his arms and hands out as far as he could, making a large circle around his body then said, "But now it ends here." I felt such joy for him. It was fascinating. It

55

felt magical the way he explained it. I said to myself, "Wow, he just got his awareness back. We just experienced him getting his awareness back. This is phenomenal!" Then I thought, "Oh my God, I helped him achieve that." I was joyfully overwhelmed in a "Wow" moment that lasted for days. It was beyond having a feeling of absolute fulfillment in my work. It remains one of my favorite moments with Gary and in my fitness career.

CHAPTER 10

NUMBNESS AND LOSS OF SENSATIONS

Changes in sensation are one of the first things that people notice when they are having a stroke, particularly numbness in the limbs on one side of the body or one side of the face. In Gary's case, he did not remember anything but waking up in the hospital unable to move his body after the stroke. He told me he could not feel parts of his face when he touched it, as well as parts of his arm, hand, leg, and foot on his right side.

I had the incredible experience of being with him when he was in the middle of an exercise and he stopped and said, "The sensation just came back in my hand." This was a "wow" moment. At this time he was about two years post stroke, and he was able to do a plank while using two BOSU® balls. He had his hands holding onto one BOSU® ball as his feet were on the other BOSU® ball balancing in a plank. He stopped and said, "My

feeling just came back in my hand." I asked him, "What do you mean?" He said, "I knew my hand was holding onto the BOSU® ball, but I never felt the sensation of touching it before now." It is hard to express how powerful and fabulous that experience was for him and for me as the trainer. We then walked to the front desk of the gym, and he got a water bottle out of the fridge and said, "I can feel the water is cold. I usually know I am holding the water bottle, but I had no idea the feeling of touching the bottle or the sensation of the hot or cold." This is known as cutaneous sensation. Cutaneous senses include touch and everything else we feel through our skin such as temperature, texture, pressure, vibration, and pain. These receptors also sense whether the surface is hot or cold. This was a monumental moment.

By this point in our work together, Gary had become very aware of his body and changes. He and I both became able to foresee that some new gain was going to be coming in the next few days. We didn't know what gain was coming, but we got to a point that we could tell something was going to change. He would feel off for a few days right before something neurological would change. It got so that in the last six months he would say, "I think something is ready to change again. I am feeling that off sensation I usually get." It was amazing.

CHAPTER 11

THE BALANCE DISC AND BOSU® BALL

I have used the balance discs with clients for almost 20 years to help strengthen the spine, core, posture, joints, and ligaments. Standing on the balance disc also stimulates the central nervous system. Clients use them to strengthen their balancing. We used them to warm up the spine with various gentle exercises while standing or kneeling on them. We would do some free weights while standing or kneeling as well. I explained to clients that we were activating and strengthening the small deep muscles around the spine and working on the core and balance. I knew we were stimulating the nervous system, but I never experienced just how much was actually taking place neurologically until the last few years when I began working with more clients with strong neurological issues. When clients made neurological changes, they were very visible. This journey with Gary was extremely educational for me because his neurological progress was fascinating to witness.

About the time Gary was going to be using the BOSU® ball I was just getting ready to go away to a fitness convention. I saw there was a BOSU® certifications available to take. I decided I want to learn more about it. I spent sessions with BOSU® when I was there and received a BOSU® Master Trainer Specialty Certification and BOSU® Ball Complete Workout System Certification. The timing was perfect. I was working with many clients with different types of neurological issues. Within the next year, I began to see a difference in neurological changes with clients as they worked on a BOSU® ball compared to the balance disc. I could not pin point why. I needed to know what was going on in the brain and nervous system that would cause a notable difference between working on the BOSU® ball versus the balance disc. Since I had the experience to see various types of significant neurological changes in clients the last few years, I began to do more research as well as I asked as many questions as I needed until I got answers that made sense. I had established communication with David Weck, the inventor of the BOSU® Ball, earlier in Gary's process. I sent him a message sharing with him various stories of clients who have had these significant changes while working with the BOSU® ball. I asked him if he could explain to me what happens differently neurologically when someone uses the disc compared to the BOSU® ball.

He explained that the disc is known as an unstable, unstable surface and the BOSU® ball is known as a stable, unstable surface. The BOSU® ball was invented to absorb the body's weight into its dome, allowing the bracing system in the body to relax. Therefore, the nerves get stimulated deeper into the nerve roots. This brought clarity as to why my clients with neuropathy, plantar fasciitis, fascia issues, and various neurological issues had shown significant, unexpected improvements when they used the BOSU® ball. Since this particular interaction, David Weck, who continues to do research with his products, has added new conclusions to working with the BOSU® ball. Now he explains that an increased muscle strength is built due to adaptation in the neurological system and the resistance through the lower body from standing on the BOSU® ball. It's not only considered a balance tool but a resistance tool. He refers to it now as a 3D pressurized, elastic resistance tool that you compress with the feet as you stand on it and do specific exercises properly.

For the first several months Gary was not able to be on the BOSU® ball because of its height and width. I needed him to be in control and stay safe while he was stepping on and off of it. His loss of spatial awareness also contributed to his not being able to easily control that right foot in his foot placement. He used the balance disc as early on as he could. It made sense in Gary's case as he worked with the balance disc as he stimulated his nervous system, I feel, it also helped his brain and body establish strengthening and communicating to the bracing system in his body. For months, Gary would point to a BOSU® ball at the gym with a big smile on his face and say, "I want to stand on that." I would tell him he would be able to soon. I am not a physical therapist nor did we have harnesses at the gym as they do in therapy facility for safety. I had to rely on him being able to step on and off safely and to hold on to the bar and maintain stability on his own to avoid falls and injuries.

Throughout the time we worked together, Gary continued to have a strong inner connection to what he needed to do next. I think at some level he knew his neurological system was ready for the BOSU® ball.

In the illustration below, Gary is at two and a half years post stroke. He is squatting up and down slowly on the BOSU®

ball as he is bouncing a basketball. In the first year of training with me, bouncing a ball was extremely frustrating for him. The coordination and hand control on the right side was not ready for such a task. As his spatial awareness, proprioception, and different cognitive skills became stronger, he was able to coordinate all the skills needed for combining the BOSU® ball and bouncing the ball. In this picture, his nervous system is being stimulated and fired up as there is resistance force going up his legs. He is balancing and coordinating where to bounce the ball and how high so he can still control his hands. There are  many amazing internal things going on. This is one of his most incredible and my favorite combination of skills in an activity he achieved. This includes spatial awareness cognitive skills to coordinate the reach to the ball, the controlling of the arm and hand to how much speed and power was needed to get the ball to bounce to the height he wanted, as well as controlling it in his space so it did not hit the BOSU® ball instead of the floor. He also balanced and performs the movement of going up and down while doing squats. This looks like it was easy for Gary, but it was not. He could do it well, but it took one hundred percent focus and concentration. He did it; then he stepped off and said, "Wow, that is hard." We worked together over two years before he was ready to work on this.

This also meant many movements and cognitive skills needed for everyday life had also developed. This achievement, as in all of them, was a foundation for the next functional gain his body was going to attain to help him in everyday activities and movements.

CHAPTER 12

LEG BRACE, FOOT DROP AND TURN OUT

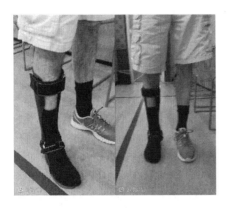

As I've mentioned, Gary had a brace on his right leg when we met. The brace was there to help keep his lower leg, ankle, and foot stable enough for walking as well as to control the foot drop and turn out. I wanted to know how his leg moved without the brace on. He was eager to take it off so we could see how he moved without it. He said he hated that thing and hoped he never had to put it back on again. I've mentioned that I am not a physical therapist, but as far as I was concerned, the brace was not going to help build any functional, structural strength needed to fix the problem. I told him my thoughts and left it to him to continue without wearing it. His determination to beat this stroke was strong even at the first few weeks of working together. He began taking the brace off when we trained and slowly faded it out completely. I do not have the exact date documented for this, but it was within the first few weeks. It was such a short time, yet it was a big step and an important piece in his recovery. Gary did not tell me until I knew him for about six months that he was told he would have to wear the brace on his leg for the rest of his life.

In this wonderful journey with Gary, I learned the vastus medialis plays an important role in the foot drop out and foot turn out that many stroke survivors end up having. In my stroke research, I read that in some cases certain strokes try to paralyze the vastus muscle group. I am not sure if this is what happened in Gary's case, but it made sense. I had a couple exercises planned for Gary to help correct this. I spoke to another fitness professional and asked him what he would do. I liked his idea better. He suggested using the leg extension machine and only perform the top 1/3 of the movement. Gary began with this the next session. In just a couple of sessions working on this, we got the foot turn out almost 50% better. It was fabulous. I was not expecting such quick results.

Gary was a grateful man and for several months he was aware that he was forgetting many things. He asked me repeatedly for weeks, "Did you tell your friend I said thank you?" I would tell him yes and that I was very thankful too. He wanted everyone who helped him to know how thankful he was. He told me that he was grateful that I was the sort of person who was willing to ask others questions to help him in his recovery.

This leg extension exercise was not an easy exercise for Gary to do. We started very light weight at 15 pounds and it was extremely difficult. He was still partially numb and very weak in the right leg, especially in this particular movement. He was able to perform it well in full range of motion, but when he had to focus on staying at the top 1/3, it was extremely tough. If I had him keep the foot from turning out and keep the toes towards him (dorsiflexion), he would say it felt like 100 pounds. This was the one exercise he did where I saw him struggle the most throughout our whole journey. He could do much more weight at this time, at almost three years post stroke, but still, if I made him position the foot dorsiflexed it felt to him like I tripled the weight resistance. In the beginning this would be the exercise we ended with in sessions because it fatigued the leg. We would do 2 to 4 sets of 8 to 10 reps. I would base it on what his energy level was that day.

This was a very challenging time in our communication to figure out fatigue, heaviness due to the stroke, or if it felt like the leg was going to collapse under him. We had a lot of laughter and long conversations as he sat in the leg extension machine. I insisted that he keep his cane with him to use after this exercise for a long time until he was able to distinguish the feeling of leg fatigue for safety precautions.

Gary and l would have some great laughs because he grew up a surfer from California, and he would put his hands on his hips and stand with his leg turned out as if he was trying to look cool. He would sit down slouching with the right leg and foot turned out. I would tell him to stop standing and sitting like a cool surfer dude because it was holding his foot in the position we are trying to fix. We would laugh and he would say, "Oh yeah, I forgot."

The body gets stronger in the movements and posture it repeats most often. When there is a foot drop and leg turn out, it puts an imbalance up to the hip and to the spine. This is just as important to understand as to knowing that having stable core and pelvis help keep the hips, knees, and feet in better alignment for best performance. He had to be conscious of what the right leg and foot were doing as often as possible. After constantly reminding him, he finally began to be aware of it on his own. At that time, he would consciously place his right foot in proper alignment whenever he remembered.

All the exercises combined helped bring his walking gait to normal. The pictures with the leg brace were taken a few months ago when Gary showed up at the gym to train one day and pulled it out of his backpack and said, "We need to have pictures of this stupid thing in the book, too." He was ecstatic that he no longer needed the leg brace, especially since he was told he would be wearing this brace the rest of his life.

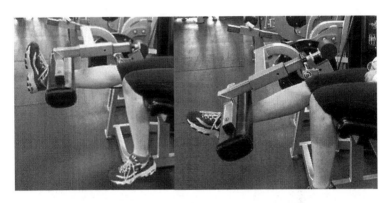

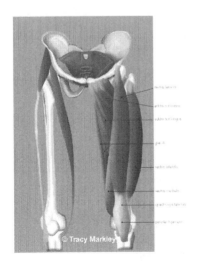 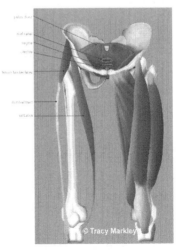

Dorsiflexion   *Plantar Flexion*

CHAPTER 13

POOR POSTURE AND ROTATOR CUFF INJURY

As an artist, Gary spent a great deal of his life with his physical posture in rounded shoulders and his head forward. This is known as Kyphosis posture, and it contributed to the rotator cuff injury he had.

We had some work to do to correct this, but it is impossible to rehab a shoulder properly if the thoracic spine and shoulder girdle are not staying in proper alignment. The stabilizing muscles of the body have to be strong enough to stabilize the rib cage, diaphragm, and thoracic spine. This proper posture is necessary to keep the shoulder girdle in proper alignment so the rotator cuff muscles can heal and rebuild correctly to keep the shoulder stable. This then leads to the head being able to stabilize in proper alignment. Poor posture causes the body to have mechanical deficiency and slow down motor control. It can cause physiological and neurological stress. Rounded shoulders and poor posture also affect the thoracolumbar fascia.

In addition, we were dealing with the effects of the stroke that left his arm feeling weak, heavy, numb, and not taking commands from the brain for movements like it used to do.

Again, I targeted the core, stabilizing, and postural muscles. We would work on the shoulder a bit, but there was not enough movement and stability to do this yet. He did go to the physical therapist for this in the beginning, but it was not working because he did not have the stability and strength in his core to hold his body upright in the correct posture to rebuild it. The body has a shoulder girdle and a shoulder joint. They are two different things. If the shoulder girdle is not held in its proper position for shoulder stabilization, the shoulder joint movement will be faulty. I wanted to build the body with proper mechanics for whole body performance and to avoid injuries now and in the future. We needed to speed up his motor control not slow it down.

After a year of working together, he had gained enough core strength and stability that when he went back to the therapist for the rotator cuff injury it had begun to heal properly. I strongly believe it was because by that time, his core was strong enough that he was able to hold his shoulder girdle in proper alignment. This allowed the therapy exercises to ultimately work.

Every day that I saw Gary, I would say to him, "Set your shoulders and stand up tall." It sometimes seemed like I had to say it every other minute. It was a habit, a structural weakness combined with having to focus on many things at once that he often had to do. Often, especially in the beginning months he would say, "Oh yeah, I forgot." Then he would try to sit up tall again. Then a few minutes later, I had to tell him again. It was tough work for him, but since we laughed a lot at ourselves while working together, it made it easier to get through. I often thought when other members of the gym could hear us they would think I was bossy.

If someone does not have strong enough stabilizing muscles to hold the body upright, the shoulders are not able to stay in proper alignment. It is biomechanics of the body. I have repeated this throughout the book because it is enormously important. It is like piling a stack of boxes on top of one another. If the bottom box is half-full and unstable, everything that stacks on top begins to sink into the bottom box. They are stacked unstable, and out of balance, therefore they are unsafe and may fall. Fortunately, Gary did not have lower back issues, and I was building his body up the best it could be so he would not develop back issues in the future. That was also very important.

When the head is balanced on the body correctly, you have better balance. If the core and rib cage are unstable, the shoulders cannot sit strongly in proper placement. Sitting on machines and working the upper back is not the cure for poor posture. It is important to strengthen the muscles at that angle as well, but there is more to it, as I just explained. It is crucial to understand muscle facilitation and recruitment patterns for the entire body. Now Gary can do planks and pushups without injury because he is exercising in the right position, which means he will remain injury free. This also means when he works his chest, biceps, and triceps, they will be in their correct position. He can attend to his everyday life the best he can without re-injuring that shoulder. He can do walking lunges with walking sticks where his muscles in his whole body work together as a team without risking injury in his shoulder. He can now do some great functional exercises and can build up healthy recruitment patterns throughout the body.

Around the time we had been working together for two years, we were in the middle of a training session. I noticed that I had not corrected him on his posture all session. He was standing up right and moving exceptionally well. He had become strong enough now that it has made him able to hold his shoulder girdle in place without constantly forcing it. It meant that any new pathways needed for him to stand up tall without thinking about it had been made. This was also the day he walked across the gym for the first time and turned around perfectly, as if he never had a stroke. After that more gains started happening more frequently.

*(Approximately two years of posture changes
shown as he is standing on the balance disc)*

CHAPTER 14

PILATES

Pilates was another added avenue for Gary in his stroke recovery. Pilates focuses on stabilizing and strengthening the center of the body to transfer power to the limbs and arms and decreases stress on ligaments and joints. It improves mental strength. Pilates flows with fluidity and grace. Pilates trains whole-body integration that reflects healthy fascia throughout the body.

PILATES

Gary added mat Pilates to his activities 17 months post stroke. He and I had been working together for about 11 months. We had been doing three, one-hour private training sessions a week. On his off days, he would come into the gym and walk on the treadmill, stand on both the balance disc and BOSU® ball, and do a few things he was able to do safely on his own. This was not too much at this point because he would not be as focused and/or he would sometimes forget to be in proper posture and form.

We discussed previously that when he was ready it would be great for him to take the mat Pilates classes that I teach. He was ready, and I suggested that he try coming to them. We also cut down to only two private sessions a week.

I told him when he got to class to sit near me so he could see and hear me. If he was close, I could still coach him to his special needs. I also told him that there would be many things that he still could not do but instead to rest and breathe. In time, he would be able to do more. He had loss of peripheral vision and a blind spot on his right side. He still struggled with getting to the floor as well as getting up off the floor, although he was doing much better than when I first met him. At the beginning, it was an extremely, difficult task; he would just fall to the floor, and it took effort and his holding onto something to get himself up. He was to the point now where it was a little struggle, but he was able to do it without the assistance of his cane or a chair. He was determined to conquer all the Pilates exercises. He began to take three mat Pilates classes a week under my guidance combined with his private training sessions. Though he could not do many of the exercises, he made an effort in every class and slowly he was able to do more. He never gave up. He rarely missed class or a day at the gym. Since his first Pilates class, he had students that rooted him on. He continued to make gains. He never gave up. This is one message Gary hoped his story would bring to others. He wanted people never to give up. In fact, the last few months in our private training sessions, out of the blue, he would stop exercising and say to me, "Let's make a deal. You never give up, and I will never give up." He would tell me not to give up on getting our story out there. He had a big heart to bring hope and encouragement to those in stroke recovery. He understood and personally experienced that with continued movement and proper direction the body can continue to heal and repair. This has not been a quick process by any means.

In Pilates, one should be focused on every movement as they flow through each exercise. I began teaching Gary to understand this mindset needed for his stroke recovery from the day we met in every exercise he did. It is difficult for many people to focus and be present when they exercise, but it is especially hard after one has a stroke. As time went on Gary would continue to do better gradually mastering some of the Pilates movements. I was so proud of him. He would struggle with certain exercises for months and then one day I would look at him in class and he had it mastered. I would say to him, "Gary, you are doing it." He would say, "I am?" I would be so happy for him, and he would get a big smile and say, "Thank you." It didn't just mean he could do an exercise when that happened; it meant his body had made a further gain in functioning properly and communicating with the brain. It's huge. At this time when new students came to class who seemed discouraged and did not know Gary had had a stroke, Gary and I would tell them how he began. They would say things like, "That's amazing. I have no excuse then." His journey has been such an inspiration to so many people. It is important to know that he added Pilates, as he continued with everything else he was doing.

After a few months in Pilates, he wanted to try to attend all the classes I taught. I told him he could try them all but yoga. I felt he was not able to hold the yoga poses. All the classes I taught are a full-body workout that focuses on building around the core. He began to come to all my classes, and he would sit right near me. The students in all my classes knew that this was his spot, and no one would take it. They always supported him. It was very special. I know he appreciated it, because he told me. As a group fitness instructor and personal trainer, I found these moments to be emotional and personal highlights in my fitness career. On the few occasions he had to miss, everyone would ask, "Where is Gary?

CHAPTER 15

PERIPHERAL VISION LOSS AND SEEING COLORS

It is common for many stroke patients to have a loss of peripheral vision on one side. I thought if all these gains and progress in Gary's condition were happening, maybe it could work as well on his peripheral vision loss as well. I spoke to a mentor of mine and he supposed that no one had tried it, so it wasn't known if it could help or not. He encouraged me to go for it and see what happened.

When we were adding visual tracking with the eyes a few minutes a couple times a week, there were a couple of times he would say he had experienced times where it was getting better. However it was a short-term fix and then it would go back to where it was. He saw his eye doctor and at times wore special glasses for this when he wasn't at the gym. I had never seen him wear them, and it wasn't something that I wanted to focus on long-term because I didn't want to interfere with any care he had from his eye doctor. There were other things to be focused on in his recovery, but it was quite a great learning experience for the both of us. His moments of improved vision may have been a fluke thing or possibly an example of what can help in some cases with the eyes.

I began by holding different objects and having him track them with his eyes as I moved the objects. Sometimes I would have him follow with his eyes without moving his head and other times moving his head. At our next visit, I grabbed items around the gym in different colors. I found things blue, red, green, purple, orange, and yellow. Gary and I then discovered he could not see colors correctly. It took at least 15 seconds to a minute before he would say a color and a couple colors were not programming in his brain at all. I then thought; let's have him stand on the balance disc. To our great surprise, his brain registered to some of the colors almost instantly.

I sent a message that evening to a highly regarded educator in the fitness industry, Peter Twist. I told him what happened, and I asked him what he thought was going on in the brain while standing on the balance disc that made the colors clear and quicker to grasp. We discussed how the central nervous system gets stimulated when the body is on unstable surfaces, as in the balance discs and BOSU® balls. He said when he is having a hard time focusing or learning a script, he stands on the BOSU® ball barefoot, and it brings his mind to clarity and focus. This helped me understand that the stimulation of the brain and the nervous system could do such a thing.

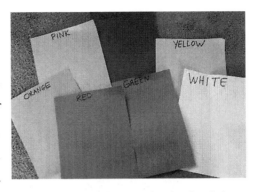

This was an experience that clearly confirmed that both of these unstable surfaces, the balance disc and the BOSU® ball stimulate the nervous system and at a level I was not aware of. This helped me understand that because of Gary's fragile state I was able to actually see and not just be aware that the nervous system was being stimulated. The next day, I brought in different colored construction paper, and we began working on seeing colors as he stood on the balance disc for 10 minutes each session. It was incredible to witness such dynamics.

At times, it was frustrating for him because he would see a color but would say a different color. Once I told him the correct color, he would explain how he knew it, but the brain was not processing the right color he wanted to say. Since he had been an artist his whole life, his brain would try to identify the exact shade of blue as we see in paint and crayons. It was definitely a lot of work with his brain.

At this time he was still working on getting quicker movements and reaction time with his arms and hands. This is when I suggested that he get the Simon® game and use it at home when he was on the disc. Simon® is an electronic memory game that came out in the 80s and is still in stores. It has four big buttons to press, and they are all different colors. The game makes a different noise with each flashing color, and you have to follow the pattern with memory. The idea was for him to stand on the balance disc and have the Simon® game to the side that was affected by the stroke. This would help stimulate his brain, help regain faster reaction time, and help his memory.

Some days we had unexpected fun with Gary having this blind spot on the right side. He could not see people if they were in that blind spot. One day he was in the hallway getting a mint out of his little mint container he had with him. He did not realize I was there until I said his name, and it startled him and the mints went flying across the gym. It was priceless. We spent the next hour in his training session laughing more than usual.

CHAPTER 16

GARY MEETS THE PARAMEDICS WHO SAVED HIS LIFE

*Matt, Ronnie and Gary the morning
they came to class*

Nearly two and a half years after his stroke, Gary attended my birthday dinner. There were about 15 of us there, and he was having a conversation with my friend's husband, Matt.

During the conversation, he found out that Matt was a paramedic in town. Gary shared his story and wanted to know who had saved his life the day he had his stroke and 911 was called. He had mentioned to me often that he would like to personally thank the paramedics who saved his life. Matt called in to check the date and see who was on that call. He looked up at Gary and said, "It was me." He was the paramedic who came to Gary's house the evening of his stroke. It was a special moment that meant a lot to Gary. He was so happy to finally be able to thank him for saving his life. This moment was such a touching moment for both of them.

As the evening ended and Gary had already left, I was speaking to Matt. He told me that he told Gary he was going to bring the other paramedic who was with him in the ambulance that transported him to the hospital over an hour away the day of his stroke, to meet him. I asked who it was and learned that it was Ronnie, another paramedic I knew. We have all talked and joked amongst one another, while at the gym, where Gary and I trained together.

I was teaching a class the next morning, which Gary attended, and we planned for both paramedics to come the class, and surprise him. They walked into class and Gary looked at him and said, "It's you? I talk to you all the time. I had no idea." He then walked over to shake his hand and say thank you. He was so touched. The class applauded and got tears in their eyes. A few said they had chills. I did as well. It meant the world to Gary. It was such an honor to be part of that whole experience.

Matt, Gary and Tracy at her birthday dinner

CHAPTER 17

A SOUL OF INSPIRATION

Gary had been making nonstop progress in his stroke recovery. I was having a hard time determining the end of the book since great gains, big and small, he kept achieving. After he got to say thank you to the paramedics, I thought that would be a good place to end this book. He agreed.

The book was almost ready to give to the editor, when one Saturday morning I received a phone call from Gary. In his happy-go-lucky voice, he said he wouldn't be making it to class that day. I asked him why. He told me he was in the hospital. He was having a hard time breathing the evening before and had to call 911. He was in good spirits and laughing. I thought he was joking at first, but he wasn't. Turns out that he needed a valve replacement in his heart. He just wanted to get it over with so he could get back to the gym and continue in his progress. He now wanted this surgery and its recovery to be the last chapter in the book.

He was in the hospital from that Saturday morning until the following Thursday when the surgery was scheduled. We spoke daily. Once he was on the phone when we were beginning one of the classes he regularly attended at the gym, and everyone got to say hello to him.

After surgery, the doctor said it all went well and he would be in recovery soon. He did not come out until several hours later because he had suffered a massive heart attack shortly after surgery. Unfortunately, after several weeks in the ICU, his family, friends, and community lost the dear man. He touched so many lives and is truly missed.

There are so many inspiring stories of Gary but one very special one was within the last year and a half. He began confidently walking up to others in the gym who he saw in a wheel chair or with a cane whom he could see had experienced a stroke. He would tell them how bad off he was after his stroke. Actually he would smile with a little chuckle and say, "I was a mess and look at me know." Then he would tell them, "Don't give up" and "Don't quit." He would explain to them that it is possible that they can get out of the wheelchair or get rid of the cane. It was exceptionally touching to watch him do this. He became like the woman who came up to him and gave him hope when he was using the walker the first day we met. After he would encourage these members he saw in the gym, he would tell me that people need to know how we did this and that he could not have done it without me. He was determined and would say to me, "I want my story shared."

I'm convinced that if he hadn't passed, he would still be making fantastic progress. He was very proud of the February article that we were in as a personal trainer and client success story. He felt the whole story needed to be told and encouraged me to finish the book as soon as possible because people need it.

His family made shirts and water bottles that said "Inspired by Gary". It has been six months since we lost Gary and I still see someone wearing one of these shirts daily around town. Recently, Russell, one of Gary's friends at the gym who was deeply inspired by him made himself and I shirts that reads "Gary said" on the front of the shirt and on the back of the shirt it reads "Never give up. Don't quit."

Russell told me Gary told him those words the first day he was in a Pilates class. Gary had been taking Pilates for about a year at that time. He noticed that Russell was having a hard time. After class Gary walked up to him, put his hand on his shoulder and said "Never give up. Don't quit."

TRIBUTE TO MY FRIEND, GARY

*Somewhere, someone out there is thinking about you and
the tremendous positive impact you have had on their life.*

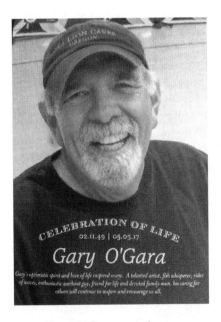

Gary O'Gara passed away
May 5, 2017 from unexpected
surgery complications.

TRIBUTE TO MY FRIEND, GARY

I lost my dear friend and fabulous client Friday evening. Gary was the kindest, most determined and inspiring person I have ever met. He was brought into my world for me to help him achieve a better life, if possible. As much as he always thanked me and was so very humble and grateful for our work and achievements together, as a team in his recovery, I always thanked him for what knowing him has done for me. He brought joy to my world both personally and professionally.

He helped bring great knowledge my way. It brought me to study and learn more about the brain and the neurological system in a way I never thought I would. I was able to meet great educators in the fitness industry by reaching out and asking questions because of this inspired journey that I was so blessed to share with him

He helped make my world bigger. I am wiser in my work.

The absolute level of joy in the achievements we experienced together were fascinating. Some days I got chills and was beyond the "Wow" moments in a great gain he would make. Some days there were tears, some days pep talks were needed but mostly "Ah" moments of great things and lots of laughter.

We experienced these spectacular moments where we both can see when the brain just made a connection to a new pathway forming a movement coming back in his stroke recovery right before our eyes. Words can't even express the power of awesomeness we both felt in those moments. How lucky I feel to have had those moments and memories.

When he got to the point where he could attend group exercise in the classes I taught, he sat right near me so I could keep a close eye on him. Everyone knew that was his spot and no one would take it. He felt loved and supported by those in the classes with us and everyone throughout the gym. Everyone cheered him on and supported him. He was tremendously grateful for this. I know this, because he frequently told me.

He brought joy to those who spoke to him, exercised near or with him and to those who just saw him across the room. Several members of his gym community have told me that just seeing him when they came into the gym made them smile and feel inspired.

This last year with me he had a strong focus to encourage and help others. We were written up in the IDEA Fitness Journal in February for his great achievements and our work together in a client success story. He was exceptionally proud of this article. It encouraged him even more to want to help others. He strongly held a passion to have more of his story shared to help others who have had a stroke. We have been working on a book of his recovery journey. He made me promise him, no matter what ever happens, to finish this project. This was said before he knew he even needed heart surgery. He had to go in for a valve replacement on his heart several weeks ago. He had some complications, and it led to more complications. Unfortunately, even with his eager determination his tired healing body could not make it through this last struggle.

He said if his story just helps one person that that one person is worth it.

He was incredible. I am definitely keeping my promise to him.

Often, the last few months out of the blue he would say to me, "Let's make a deal you never give up and I will never give up." I won't ever forget that.

I will always be a better person for knowing him. I will never forget all I learned from him and with him both professionally and personally. There is obvious a big void in my heart and my work space right now. Thank you to all my supporters.

A cool thing happened. Friday afternoon I received my May 2017 IDEA Fitness Journal in the mail. I opened it up and saw an article called, When Students Grieve. It was about grieving the loss of a client and fellow gym students grieving the loss as well. I got the call that Gary passed away just a few hours after reading this. This timing was a blessing and just goes to show how powerful and special Gary's journey was.

I am so proud of him and will forever be so very proud of him. I see him smiling up in heaven balancing on the clouds like they are BOSU® balls with a big smile on his face, out of pain and wishing all of us who are grieving him joy and happiness and to never give up!!

Rest in peace, dear Gary.

You made a tremendous positive impact in my life.

Thank you.

Russell happily admires Gary's artwork

Russell and Tracy wearing our special shirts

Suzanne, Phil and Ada at Pilates class

Cristine and Belle
smiling for Gary

Gary's loving sister and
brother-in-law,
Cheryle and Jeffrey

Cheryle and Tracy proudly
showing their water bottles

Lee and Wasabi appreciate all
that Gary has done for Tracy

THE STROKE OF AN ARTIST

Lovely Essie, 104 years old, making a muscle for Gary

One of Gary's biggest fans and friend, Carol

Gary, his friend, Jim and Jim's brother showing the IDEA article

Tracy and Todd Durkin with Gary's water bottle

Eve, who cheered Gary on during the 300 classes she shared with him

TRIBUTE TO MY FRIEND, GARY

*Russell wearing
Gary's shirt*

*John, who was always
a help to Gary*

Carol and Gary practicing their finger exercises

*Russell and Phil after a
Pilates session*

*Tracy and Russell in front
of Gary's favorite piece of
equipment, the BOSU® Ball*

ACKNOWLEDGEMENTS

A big, loving thank you to Cheryle, Gary's sister, for being such a loving and caring sister to Gary and bringing him to the gym with hopes he can make more progress.

A very special thank you to Gary for trusting me. I like to thank you for not giving up on yourself and for being so very dedicated to your recovery every day. Your journey and story has brought inspiration, joy, encouragement, and knowledge to myself and others.

A big thank you to Susan, my incredible illustrator who walked into the gym like a miracle. As this book was in progress, I wanted to include muscle illustrations. I tried to draw some myself. I have absolutely no skill in drawing, especially muscles. One day Susan came into the gym to meet with me to discuss an exercise program. She understood quite well when I talked about muscles and the body. I said to her, "Were you a nurse? You really understand the body." She answered "No, I was an illustrator of muscles and anatomy for nursing books for 25 years. Why, do you need my services? I want to volunteer my time." I responded,

"Are you serious?" She said, "Yes." I said, "I cannot believe you just said that to me." Then I told her about the book. She meant what she said. I was beyond excited. I went over to her house the next day to see her work. It was amazing. She told me to tell her what I wanted and she would make them for me. When I told Gary about our meeting he was shocked. He said, "Do you know how hard it is to find artists who can do that kind of work and then for her to walk into this gym, in this small town and come to you out of the blue?" It was incredible, like her work. This was another unique experience that was part of the great journey with Gary's recovery.

Thank you to Maire, Cathy, Tammy, Dawnielle and Melissa for volunteering and doing trades with me by helping with editing and photography.

I would like to thank all of my teachers I have learned from in the past 20 years. A special thank you to David Weck, for our insightful chats and for inventing the BOSU® ball. Without this tool, Gary would not have made the ongoing great progress physically and neurologically that he did.

Thank you to Facebook and Instagram for having these platforms to share Gary's videos and pictures to so others could be inspired and encouraged as they wrote wonderful comments that I would read to Gary. They gave him joy and inspiration.

Thank you to my mom and step-father, Lee for helping me get to Florence and all you have done for me. I would not have had this experience if I hadn't been here.